Sam's painting

Story by Joan Jarden
Illustrations by Pat Reynolds

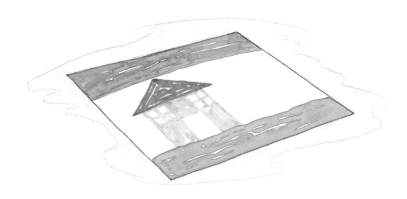

One day, Sam did a big painting.

She painted some green grass.

She painted a yellow house
with a red roof.

Sam painted some blue at the top for the sky.

Her painting looked beautiful.

"Now I'm going to paint
the sun in the sky,"
said Sam.

"But I can't!" she said.
"The blue paint is too wet.
The yellow paint will run into it."

"My painting will dry in the sun,"
said Sam,
and she went outside with it.

But Sam's painting
went flying away in the wind.

"Oh, help!" she shouted.

Sam's painting came down
in the wet mud.

"Oh, no! My painting!" said Sam,
and she ran to get it.

Sam looked at the mud
on her painting.

"It's no good now," she said.

But then Sam
looked at her painting again.

"The mud looks like a brown dog," said Sam.

"Mom, it looks like Bingo! I can see his tail."

Sam painted two ears and two eyes and a black nose on the dog.

"Look, Bingo!" said Sam.

"My painting is **very** beautiful

with you in it."